BIG BOOBS IS...

BY KELLI GEORGE

Illustrations by ED POWERS

PRICE/STERN/SLOAN
Publishers, Inc., Los Angeles
1981

Dedicated to Marianne and Jamie

FIFTH PRINTING — SEPTEMBER 1981

Copyright© 1979 by Kelli George
Illustrations Copyright© 1979 by Price/Stern/Sloan Publishers, Inc.
Published by Price/Stern/Sloan Publishers, Inc.
410 North La Cienega Boulevard, Los Angeles, California 90048

Printed in the United States of America. All rights reserved. No part of this publication may be reproduced, stored in a retrieval system, or transmitted, in any form or by any means, electronic, mechanical, photocopying, recording, or otherwise, without the prior written permission of the publishers.
ISBN: 0-8431-0473-2

PSS!® is a registered trademark of Price/Stern/Sloan Publishers, Inc.

Some people may call the following material gross. These people have never walked around as a 38-DD. I hope, after reading the following insights, there will be a little less snickering and a little more understanding of those with . . . BIG BOOBS!

—Kelli George

BIG BOOBS IS

... being recognized

BEFORE

you turn the corner!

... always having a gap between the second and third buttons.

BIG BOOBS IS

. . . having a bigger bra than your 6th grade teacher.

. . . trying the pencil test
(to see if you need a bra)
and finding out
you can use a
typewriter!

BIG BOOBS IS

. . . reading a book in bed and not getting tired arms.

. . . never taking trampoline in gym class.

BIG BOOBS IS

... never being able to do pushups!

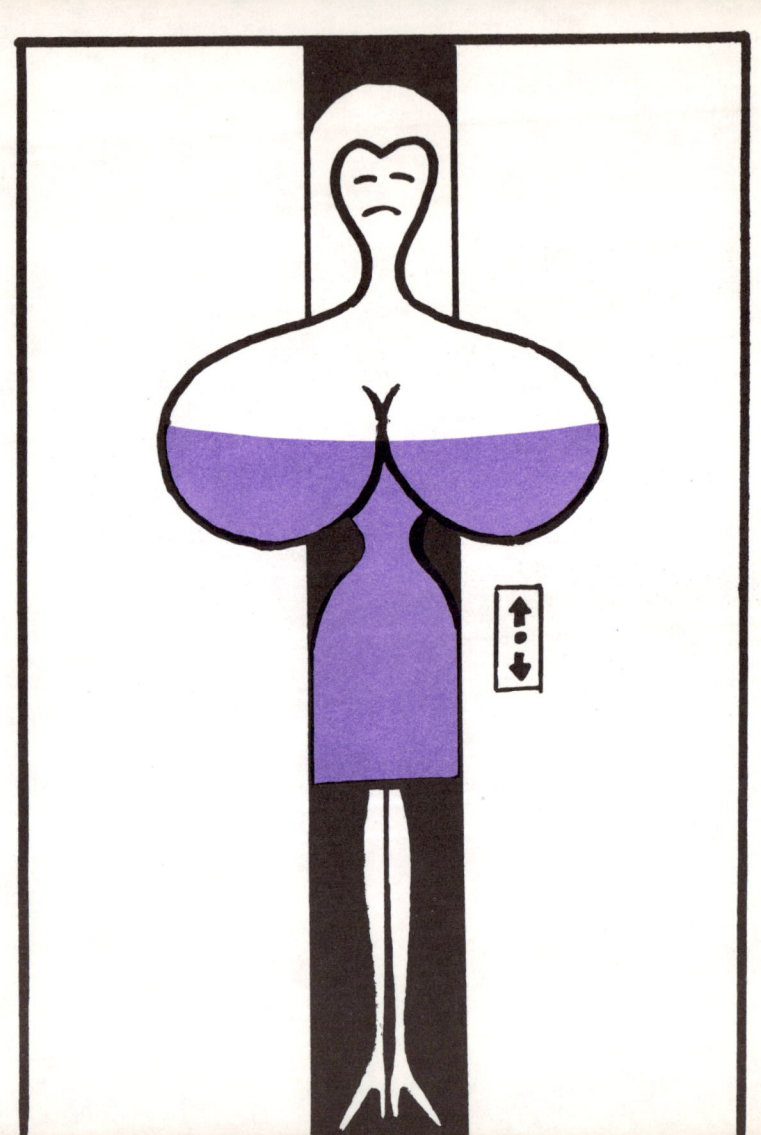

. . . being the last one in a crowded elevator
and
keeping the doors from closing.

BIG BOOBS IS

. . . going to a buffet dinner and managing beautifully when they run out of plates.

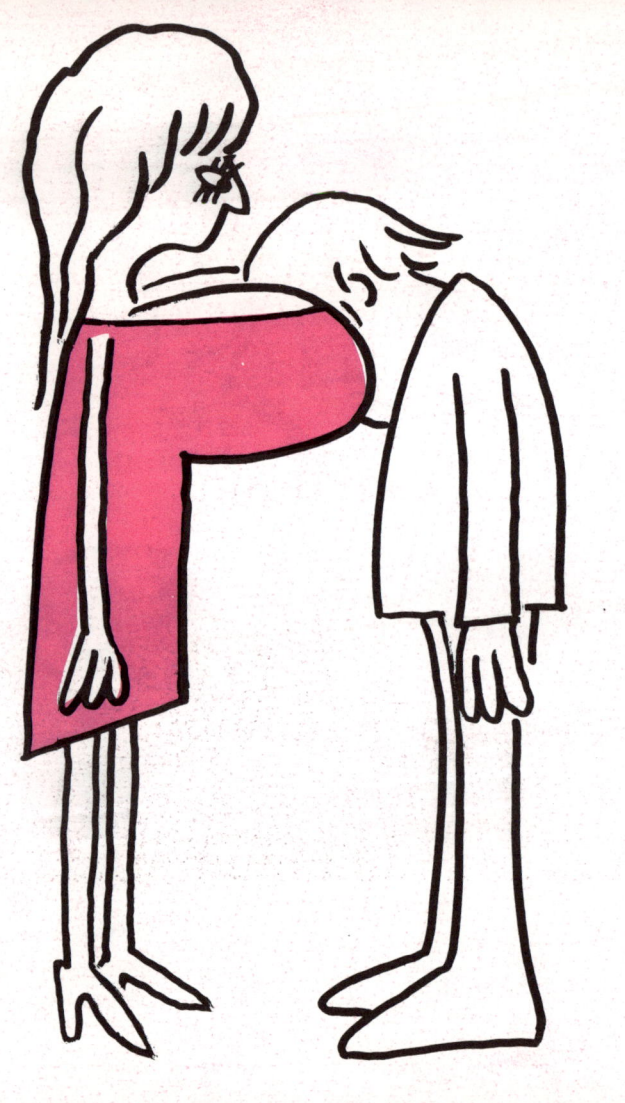

BIG BOOBS IS

...never being able to see men's eyes

... not worrying about losing your pendant if the chain breaks.

BIG BOOBS IS

. . . having to excavate BEFORE you lie on your stomach.

This book is published by

PRICE/STERN/SLOAN
Publishers, Inc., Los Angeles

whose other unusual and provocative titles
include such classics as:

SAM, THE CEILING NEEDS PAINTING ($1.50)
SEX BY THE NUMBERS ($1.50)
SEX WAS MORE FUN WHEN ($1.50)
GUILT WITHOUT SEX ($1.75)
THE WORLD'S WORST SHOW ME JOKES ($1.50)
THE TOILET BOOK ($1.50)
X-RATED RIDDLES ($1.75)

They are available wherever books are sold, or may
be ordered directly from the publisher by sending
check or money order for the full price of each title
plus $1.00 for handling and mailing. For a complete
list ot titles send a *stamped, self-addressed envelope* to:

PRICE/STERN/SLOAN *Publishers, Inc.*
410 North La Cienega Boulevard, Los Angeles, California 90048